LOOK! THAT MAN'S GIVING ANOTHER MAN A CIGARETTE! DO YOU SUPPOSE IT'S **REALLY** A CIGARETTE?

LISTEN, YOU WORRY WARTS! I CAME OVER HERE TO HAVE **FUN**! NOW SHUT UP ABOUT SPIES!

COULD A SPY HAVE A MESSAGE ROLLED UP IN A CIGARETTE?

YOU KIDS WILL DRIVE ME NUTS! FIGURE OUT THE SPY BUSINESS YOURSELVES! I WANTA BE ALONE!

AH! BEAUTIFUL SCENERY AND — AH — BEAUTIFUL SCENERY! THIS IS THE LIFE FOR ME!

FOR ONCE I'M GOING TO MIND MY OWN BUSINESS AND NOT GET INVOLVED IN ANY TROUBLE!

NEARBY!

CURSES! COUNTER-SPIES ARE ON MY TRAIL! HOW AM I GOING TO GET THIS MESSAGE TO MY FELLOW-SPY, THE ILLUSTRIOUS MADAME TRIPLE-X?

I WILL HAVE TO TRUST THE MESSAGE TO SOME STUPID PASSER-BY! **WHOM** SHALL IT BE?

DONALD IS SOMEWHAT SHOCKED!

MY STARS! THAT'S THE LIPSTICK **I** HANDED TO THAT GIRL!

AND TO THINK IT HAD A MESSAGE IN IT—!

READ THE MESSAGE, UNCA DONALD!

IT SAYS: "MADAME TRIPLE-X, DELIVER STOLEN PLANS OF U.S. Q-BOMB TO OPERATOR 4-X IN CHILIBURGERIA—

"OPERATOR 4-X IS KNOWN TO THE WORLD AS DONALDO EL QUACKO, THE BULL FIGHTER"!

BOYS, THIS **IS** SERIOUS!

LET'S TELL THE POLICE!

NO! THIS CASE IS **TOO BIG** FOR POLICE!

HOW ABOUT THE F.B.I.? COULDN'T YOU SEND THEM A CABLEGRAM?

NO! THE CABLE LINES MIGHT BE TAPPED BY SPIES!

WOW! IS IT **THAT** BAD?

WE HAVE TO BE SUSPICIOUS OF **EVERYBODY** AND **EVERYTHING**!

BOYS, THE **ONLY** THING WE CAN DO IS GET TO CHILIBURGERIA AND HIJACK THOSE PLANS!

WHERE IS CHILIBURGERIA?

IN A COUNTRY WEST OF HERE! PACK UP, AND MAKE IT SNAPPY!

So—

UNCA DONALD, WON'T MADAME TRIPLE-X BE TAKING THIS TRAIN TO CHILIBURGERIA, TOO?

COULD BE! I'M HOPING—

WABONS-LITS

NICE
MARSEILLE
BARCELONA
VALENCIA
GRANADA
SEVILLE

IF SHE DOES, WE MAY GET A CHANCE TO SEARCH HER BAGGAGE! I HOPE! I HOPE!

LATER!

THE TRAIN IS PULLING OUT, AND WE DIDN'T SEE MADAME TRIPLE-X COME ABOARD!

IT'S OKAY IF SHE COMES ON A LATER TRAIN!

WE'LL GET THERE **FIRST** AND SET A TRAP FOR HER!

TRANS EUROPE AIR

OR WILL WE?

LATER THE DUCKS AWAKEN!

I'LL BE DOGGONED! A TRAIN STANDING HERE **DESERTED**!

HUH?

IT SURE **IS** DESERTED!

NO CREWMEN ANYWHERE — NOT A PASSENGER, EITHER!

THAT MAKES ME **MAD**! HERE WE WANT TO GET TO CHILIBURGERIA AS **FAST** AS WE CAN, AND THAT TRAIN—

WAIT, NOW! DO WE HAVE TO BE **THIS** HONEST?

WE'RE TRYING TO **SAVE** OUR COUNTRY—REMEMBER?

YEAH! WHAT'RE WE **WALKING** FOR?

So—

I GUESS I PULL THIS THING! I'VE SEEN 'EM DO IT IN THE MOVIES!

CHUFF!

PULL IT MORE! WE'RE **MOVING**!

YIPPEE! IF WE GET UP ENOUGH SPEED, WE MAY EVEN BEAT MADAME TRIPLE-X TO CHILIBURGERIA!

KIDS, SHE'LL HAVE TO BE **MILES** AHEAD TO GET THERE BEFORE WE DO!

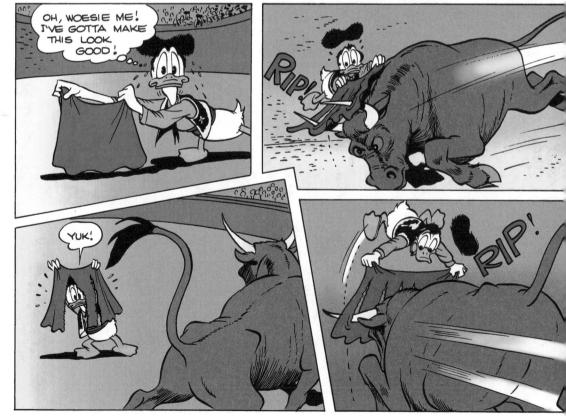

© 2005 Disney
Enterprises Inc.

The Life and Times
of
Scrooge McDuck
by
Don Rosa

We all wonder how Carl Barks' webfooted tycoon acquired his famous fortune—and in *Uncle Scrooge* 285-296 (1994-96), modern-day duck maestro Don Rosa told us in a legendary epic serial. From Scrooge's Scottish childhood to his worldwide quest for gold; from his ill-starred love life to his meetings with history's heroes, Rosa left no stone unturned, no penny unpinched. And now Gemstone Publishing is collecting all twelve Eisner-winning chapters in one 264-page trade paperback, annotated by Rosa himself and embellished with art never before seen in the United States. Look for it this June at your favorite book store or comic shop; at just $16.99, it's a deal even a tightwad could love.

Dangerous Disguise Poster
by Don Rosa

WALT DISNEY presents The Li'l BAD WOLF and THE PIGMY PIGS

WHILLIKERS! IT SEEMS LIKE I WAS SUPPOSED TO BRING BACK SOMETHING FROM THE VILLAGE... BUT I DON'T REMEMBER WHAT IT WAS!

I GOT SO INTERESTED AT THE LIBRARY THAT I COMPLETELY FORGOT!

WELL... WHERE IS IT?

WHERE IS WHAT, POP?

WHERE IS WHAT? WHY... WHAT YOU WENT TO THE VILLAGE FOR, OF COURSE!

NOW YOU'VE GOT ME SO CONFUSED, I FORGOT MYSELF WHAT IT WAS I SENT YA FOR!

I HEAR SOMETHING... MAYBE IT'S POP!

WHILLIKERS! IT'S A PIGMY PIG! I MUST FIND POP AND WARN HIM!

OH, DEAR! THERE HE IS... SURROUNDED BY A WHOLE GROUP OF PIGMIES!

POP! COME AWAY FROM THERE QUICKLY! THOSE LI'L PIGS AREN'T LIKE THE ONES YOU'VE BEEN CHASING FOR YEARS...

THESE PIGS ARE FEROCIOUS!

NOW HE TELLS ME!

WOGGA-WOGGA WUMP OG... HAT HAT!

WHA?

UH, OH! THAT SENTRY SPOTTED ME... AND NOW THEY'RE COMING AFTER ME!

Walt Disney's **UNCLE SCROOGE** *Brig-a-dog*

IT'S A FINE SUMMER'S DAY IN A BUSTLING SCOTTISH TOWN, BUT POOR DONALD'S NOT FEELING THE FUN BECAUSE HE'S ON THE JOB FOR...

MY DEAR UNCLE SCROOGE! I SHOULD'VE KNOWN ANY WORKING HOLIDAY OF HIS WOULD BE HEAVY ON THE *WORKING!*

M°DUCK TARTANS

ARDPATRICK ANNUAL DOG SHOW

2002-159

HURRY UP, NEPHEW! THIS IS ONE OF SCOTLAND'S BIGGEST *DOG SHOWS*— THE PERFECT PLACE TO UNLOAD ALL OF THE OLD *TARTANS* THAT I BOUGHT ON *EBAY!*

≠GROAN!≠ I'M SO TIRED OF LUGGING AROUND ALL THIS STUFF THAT I'M SEEING *TARTANS* EVERYWHERE— EVEN IN MY DREAMS!

M°DUCK TARTANS

I CAN'T WAIT TO CHECK IN AT THE HOTEL!

WHAT HOTEL?

YOU *DIDN'T* BOOK ANY ROOMS?

THEY ALL JACKED UP THEIR PRICES BECAUSE OF THE *SHOW!*

LOOKS LIKE WE *WALK*, LADS!

WE'LL NEVER FIND THE HOTEL OR ANYTHING *ELSE* IN THIS MESS!

WAIT! I THINK I *HEAR* SOMETHING IN THE DISTANCE!

IT LOOKS LIKE A VILLAGE!

MAYBE WE CAN GET SOME HELP!

WHO ARE THEY?

AND *WHAT* ARE THEY DOING HERE?

OCH, IT'S THAT TIME AGAIN! *WE'RE BACK!*

Huh?

THE LAST TIME "BRIG-A-DOG"— OUR VILLAGE— CAME OUT OF THIS FOG WAS EXACTLY *100 YEARS AGO!*

100... AM I LOONY FROM THE FOG?

I SEE THIS NEEDS EXPLAINING! HUNDREDS...

"...OF YEARS AGO, OUR VILLAGE WAS CELEBRATING MID-SUMMER'S EVE! EVERY-ONE WAS AS HAPPY AS COULD BE ON THAT PERFECT DAY!

"SO SOMEONE MADE A WISH THAT WE COULD ALWAYS STAY THAT WAY FOREVER!

TWEET! TWEET!

"A LOCAL DRUID WIZARD OVERHEARD AND GRANTED THE WISH!"

SINCE THEN, WE'VE HAD A *GLORIOUS* TIME!

BRIG-A-DOG *REAPPEARS* OUT OF THE MYSTIC FOG EVERY 100 YEARS FOR ONE SHORT HOUR... SO VILLAGERS CAN REJOIN THE OUTSIDE WORLD IF THEY CHOOSE! BUT, SO FAR, NO ONE HAS EVER *WANTED* TO LEAVE!

HELP ME RESCUE MY *FRIEND!*

DOES THIS MEAN THAT IF WE DON'T GET HIM BACK BEFORE THE VILLAGE VANISHES...

...YOU WON'T SEE HIM FOR ANOTHER *100* YEARS— IF *EVER?*

AND WE HAVE LESS THAN AN *HOUR* TO FIND THAT ROTTEN CROOK!

SORRY, CALLUM! IT'S TOO MUCH OF A CHANCE FOR US TO *TAKE!*

IF WE DIDN'T GET *BACK* IN TIME, WE'D BE STRANDED IN THE *OUTSIDE* WORLD!

I KNOW! BUT HAMISH WOULD DO IT FOR *ME!*

BUT YOU MIGHT NEVER SEE YOUR FAMILY OR FRIENDS AGAIN!

BUT HAMISH *IS* MY FAMILY AND MY BEST *FRIEND!*

WHAT A *BRAVE* LAD! LEAD THE WAY... WE'RE RIGHT BEHIND YOU!

BUT WE GOTTA BE CAREFUL WE DON'T GET *LOST* IN THE FOG!

GOOD THING I KNOW HOW TO *FOLLOW* A TRAIL!

LOOK! FOOTPRINTS AND SOME BROKEN TWIGS!

THIS TREE HAS *TEETH MARKS!* IT MUST BE HAMISH!

THE WEE POOCH MUST HAVE TRIED TO HANG ON—AND FAILED!

STOP!

NO! I'M SURE THIS IS THE RIGHT WAY!

WE'RE GOING FURTHER AND FURTHER AWAY FROM THE VILLAGE! EVEN IF WE FIND HAMISH, YOU MAY NOT BE ABLE TO GET BACK IN TIME!

AND EVEN WORSE— WE'VE LOST THE TRAIL!

I THINK *THIS* IS THE WAY BACK!

NO... THIS IS!

I DON'T CARE ABOUT THAT— I'VE *GOT* TO FIND HAMISH!

HOW CAN WE FIND HAMISH? WE'RE LOST *OURSELVES!*

get a DOUBLE DIP OF FUN!

It's FREE!

Every week Scoop - the free e-newsletter - serves up a heaping double dip of comic character twins. From Heckle and Jeckle to the Wonder Twins to Mary-Kate and Ashley Olsen. Just log onto http://scoop.diamondgalleries.com to subscribe. Scoop spoons up two times as much trendy, tasty tidbits as any other pop culture site. It's just dripping with news, collectible info, and fun facts!

SCOOP- IT'S INFORM LICIOUS . . AND IT'S FAT-FREE!

WALT DISNEY
CHIP 'N' DALE in OUT WEST

MOVING OUT WEST GOOD IDEA, CHIP! PLENTY NUTS HERE!

YEH, YEH! WILD 'N' WOOLY WEST MORE *NUTTY* THAN WILD 'N' WOOLY, THOUGH!

HEY! WHAT THAT OVER ENTRANCE TO OUR TREE HOME?

GASP!

REWARD

BLACK PETE

IT A MEANY MAN ON THE LOOSE!

HE SURE LOOK SCARY!

WE DON'T WORRY BOUT HIM---HE JUST ROB BANKS!

YEH! HE NOT NUT ROBBER!

CND 10-05

MEANWHILE, NEARBY...

NOW TO GET TO MY FAVORITE HIDING PLACE!

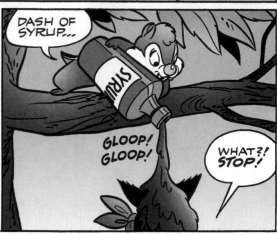

BUT HOURS LATER...

HEPZIBAH? OH, HEPZIBAH? PLEASE, HEPZIBAH...AREN'T YOU HERE?

PICKLING PARK

THIS IS THE MISSING PERSONS BUREAU, DUCKY! WE CAN'T LOOK FOR PIGEONS!

I UNDERSTAND, OFFICER! I MIGHT AS WELL GO BACK TO THE FARM AND FACE THE MUSIC!

I HATE TO THINK WHAT GRANDMA DUCK WILL SAY TO ME WHEN I HAVE TO TELL HER THAT...

YOU'RE *NOT LOST!* NOTHING HAPPENED! YOU'RE HERE! *SAFE!*

COO!

WERE YOU... A LITTLE BIT LOST?

COO!

ALL RIGHT! I GET IT! WHY WALK HOME WHEN YOU CAN GET A RIDE, YOU FIGURED! AND I RUN ALL OVER MAKING A NUMBSKULL, NUMBHEADED, LAMEBRAIN FOOL OF MYSELF!

?

HEH! TELL YOU WHAT, HEPPIE! I WON'T TELL GRANDMA DUCK, IF YOU DON'T!

COO!

BUT SOME DISTANCE AHEAD, AN OLD MOOSE STEPS OUT OF THE FOREST AND...

...DECIDES TO SHARPEN HIS HORNS ON THE HANDY POLE...

RUB!

SCRAPE!

SCRATCH!

...ACCIDENTALLY POINTING THE SIGN THE *WRONG* WAY!

HONK! HONK!

?

OOOH... LOOK AT THE MOOSE, UNCA MICKEY!

GUESS WE *SCARED* HIM!

AH! HERE'S THE SIGN! WE TAKE THE ROAD TO THE LEFT AND IT'S ONLY FIVE MILES!

BUT HOURS LATER...

THIS ROAD'S AWFULLY STEEP AND WE'VE GONE MORE THAN FIVE MILES!

IT'S GETTIN' DARK, TOO!

MOMENTS LATER...

DOGGONE IT, THE HEADLIGHTS WON'T WORK! WE'D BETTER CAMP FOR THE NIGHT, GOOFY!

OKAY, MICKEY!

THIS HERE'S A NICE SPOT, MICKEY!

GOOD! PITCH THE TENT AND WE'LL ALL TURN IN!

GOSH! I CAN'T SEE A THING!

I DON'T WANT TO.. I'M TOO SLEEPY!

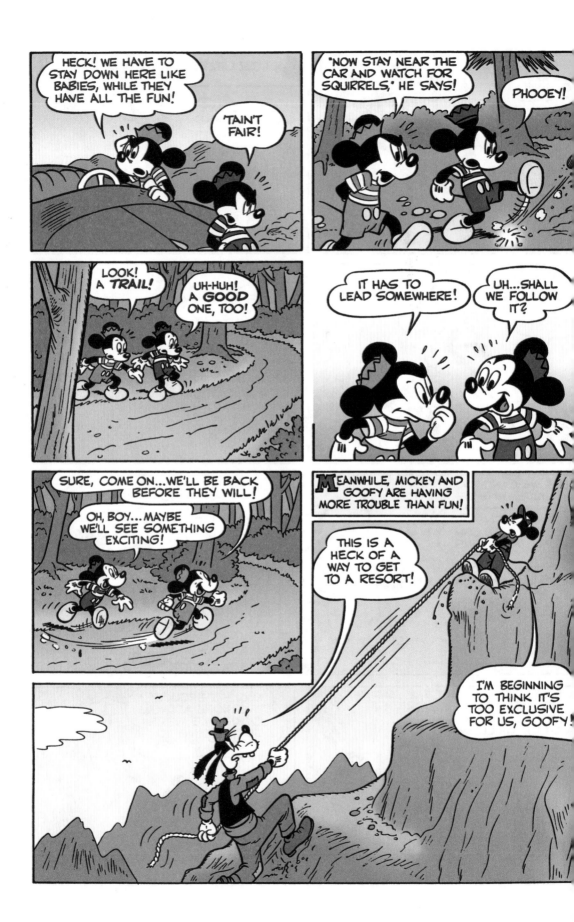

THANKS TO A HARD-HEADED BEAST...MICKEY GETS HIS WISH IN SHORT ORDER!